The Polish Americans

Consulting Editors

THE IMMIGRANT EXPERIENCE

The Polish Americans

Sean Dolan

Sandra Stotsky, General Editor
Harvard University Graduate School of Education

CHELSEA HOUSE PUBLISHERS

New York • Philadelphia

CHELSEA HOUSE PUBLISHERS

Editorial Director: Richard Rennert
Executive Managing Editor: Karyn Gullen Browne
Copy Chief: Robin James
Picture Editor: Adrian G. Allen
Creative Director: Robert Mitchell
Art Director: Joan Ferrigno
Production Manager: Sallye Scott

THE IMMIGRANT EXPERIENCE

Editors: Mary B. Sisson and Reed Ueda

Staff for THE POLISH AMERICANS

Assistant Editor: Annie McDonnell
Copy Editor: Apple Kover
Assistant Designer: Stephen Schildbach
Cover Illustrator: Jane Sterrett

First Printing

1   3   5   7   9   8   6   4   2

Library of Congress Cataloging-in-Publication Data

Dolan, Sean.
    The Polish Americans / Sean Dolan.
    p. cm.—(The immigrant experience)
    Includes bibliographical references (p.) and index.
    Summary: discusses the history, culture, and religion of the Polish, factors encouraging their emigration, and their acceptance as an ethnic group in North America.
    ISBN 0-7910-3364-3.
        0-7910-3386-4 (pbk.)
1. Polish Americans–Juvenile literature. [1. Polish Americans.] I. Title. II. Series.
E184. P7D65 1996   95–30995
973'.049185–dc20   CIP
                                                                         AC

CONTENTS

THE IMMIGRANT EXPERIENCE

CHELSEA HOUSE PUBLISHERS

A
NATION OF
NATIONS

Daniel Patrick Moynihan

The Constitution of the United States begins: "We the People of the United States. . ." Yet, as we know, the United States was not then and is not now made up of a single group of people. It is made up of many peoples. Immigrants and bondsmen from Europe, Asia, Africa, and Central and South America came here or were brought here, and still they come. They forged one nation and made it their own. More than 100 years ago, Walt Whitman expressed this great central fact of America: "Here is not merely a nation, but a teeming Nation of nations."

Although the ingenuity and acts of courage of these immigrants, our ancestors, shaped the North American way of life, we sometimes take their contributions for granted. This fine series, *The Peoples of North America*, examines the experiences and contributions of different immigrant groups and how these contributions determined the future of the United States and Canada.

Immigrants did not abandon their ethnic traditions when they reached the shores of North America. Each ethnic group had its own customs and traditions, and each brought different experiences, accomplishments, skills, values, styles of dress, and tastes in food that lingered long after its arrival. Yet this profusion of differences created a singularity, or bond, among the immigrants.

The United States and Canada are unusual in this respect. Whereas religious and ethnic differences have sparked intolerance throughout the rest of the world—from the 17th-century religious wars to the 19th-century nationalist movements in Europe to the near extermination of the Jewish people under Nazi Germany—North Americans have struggled to learn how to respect each other's differences and live in harmony.

Our two countries are hardly the only two in which different groups must learn to live together. There is no nation of significant size anywhere in the world which would not be classified as multi-ethnic. But only in North America are there so *many* different groups, most of them living cheek by jowl with one another.

This is not easy. Look around the world. And it has not always been easy for us. Witness the exclusion of Chinese immigrants, and for practical purposes Japanese also, in the late 19th century. But by the late 20th century, Chinese and Japanese Americans were the most successful of all the groups recorded by the census. We have had prejudice aplenty, but it has been resisted and recurrently overcome.

The remarkable ability of Americans to live together as one people was seriously threatened by the issue of slavery. Thousands of settlers from the British Isles had arrived in the colonies as indentured servants, agreeing to work for a specified number of years on farms or as apprentices in return for passage to America and room and board. When the first Africans arrived in the then-British colonies during the 17th century, some colonists thought that they too should be treated as indentured servants. Eventually, the question of whether the Africans should be treated as indentured, like the English, or as slaves who could be owned for life was considered in a Maryland court. The court's calamitous decree held that blacks were slaves bound to a lifelong servitude, and so also were their children. America went through a time of moral examination and civil war before it finally freed African slaves and their descendants. The principle that all people are created equal had faced its greatest challenge and survived.

Yet the court ruling that set blacks apart from other races fanned flames of discrimination that burned long after slavery was abolished—and that still flicker today. Indeed, it was about the time of the American Civil War that European theories of evolution were turned to the service of ranking different peoples by their presumed distance from our apelike ancestors.

When the Irish flooded American cities to escape the famine in Ireland, the cartoonists caricatured the typical "Paddy" (a common term for Irish immigrants) as an apelike creature with jutting jaw and sloping forehead.

By the 20th century, racism and ethnic prejudice had given rise to virulent theories of a Northern European master race. When Adolf Hitler came to power in Germany in 1933, he popularized the notion of an Aryan race. Only a man of the deepest ignorance and evil could have done this. *Aryan* is a Sanskrit word, which is to say the ancient script of what we now think of as India. It means "noble" and was adopted by linguists—notably by a fine German scholar, Max Müller—to denote the Indo-European family of languages. Müller was horrified that anyone could think of it in terms of race, especially a race of blond-haired, blue-eyed Teutons. But the Nazis embraced the notion of a master race. Anyone with darker and heavier features was considered inferior. Buttressed by these theories, the German Nazi state from 1933 to 1945 set out to destroy European Jews, along with Poles, Gypsies, Russians, and other groups considered inferior. It nearly succeeded. Millions of these people were murdered.

The tragedies brought on by ethnic and racial intolerance throughout the world demonstrate the importance of North America's efforts to create a society free of prejudice and inequality.

A relatively recent example of the New World's desire to resolve ethnic friction nonviolently is the solution that the Canadians found to a conflict between two ethnic groups. A long-standing dispute as to whether Canadian culture was properly English or French resurfaced in the mid-1960s, dividing the peoples of the French-speaking Province of Quebec from those of the English-speaking provinces. Relations grew tense, then bitter, then violent. The Royal Commission on Bilingualism and Biculturalism was established to study the growing crisis and to propose measures to ease the tensions. As a result of the commission's recommendations, all official documents and statements from the national government's capital at Ottawa are now issued in both French and English, and bilingual education is encouraged.

The year 1980 marked a coming of age for the United States's ethnic heritage. For the first time, the U.S. Bureau of the Census asked people about their ethnic background. Americans chose from more than 100 groups, including French Basque, Spanish Basque, French Canadian, African-American, Peruvian, Armenian, Chinese, and Japanese. The ethnic group with the largest response was English (49.6 million). More than 100 million Americans claimed ancestors from the British Isles, which includes England, Ireland, Wales, and Scotland. There were almost as many Germans (49.2 million) as English. The Irish-American population (40.2 million) was third, but the next-largest ethnic group, the African-Americans, was a distant fourth (21 million). There was a sizable group of French ancestry (13 million) as well as of Italian (12 million). Poles, Dutch, Swedes, Norwegians, and Russians followed. These groups, and other smaller ones, represent the wondrous profusion of ethnic influences in North America.

Canada too has learned more about the diversity of its population. Studies conducted during the French/English conflict showed that Canadians were descended from Ukrainians, Germans, Italians, Chinese, Japanese, native Indians, and Inuit, among others. Canada found it had no ethnic majority, although nearly half of its immigrant population had come from the British Isles. Canada, like the United States, is a land of immigrants for whom mutual tolerance is a matter of reason as well as principle. But note how difficult this can be in practice, even for persons of manifest goodwill.

The people of North America are the descendants of one of the greatest migrations in history. And that migration is not over.

Koreans, Vietnamese, Nicaraguans, Cubans, and many others are heading for the shores of North America in large numbers. This mix of cultures shapes every aspect of our lives. To understand ourselves, we must know something about our diverse ethnic ancestry. Nothing so defines the North American nations as the motto on the Great Seal of the United States: *E Pluribus Unum*—Out of Many, One. ⮬

On the Fourth of July, Polish Americans pose with their homemade float on Main Street in Nanticoke, Pennsylvania.

FROM POLAND TO POLONIA

Once I thought to write a history of the immigrants in America. Then I discovered that the immigrants were American history.

—Oscar Handlin

Immigrants from Poland have been living in the United States for a long time—since before the loose confederation of English colonies formally joined together to form a single political entity in the 18th century. The great Polish migration occurred in the 19th and early 20th centuries, when more than 2.5 million Poles reached American shores. Today, the 8 million people in the United States who claim Polish ancestry represent one of the nation's largest ethnic groups. They came, they created a new world for themselves, and they thrived. In their homeland, many had been peasant farmers, near the bottom of the socioeconomic ladder. From humble beginnings they moved into American communities and created an important new part of Polonia, as the Polish communities outside of Poland came to be collectively known.

13

A Polish immigrant stands dressed in Old World garb, c. 1900.

The Dream of America

The United States seemed like a haven to Polish immigrants. For intellectual refugees from the oppressive foreign and Communist governments that have dominated Poland for much of its history, the United States offered political freedom, where social issues and ideas could be discussed without the fear of persecution. For the impoverished peasants who arrived around the turn of the century and formed the bulk of Polish immigration, America offered something even more precious—a chance to get ahead, to support a family in something approaching comfort. The majority of these immigrants had planned not to settle permanently in the New World but rather to make money to take home to Poland. But the Polish economy was in a long-standing decline and the standard of living was noticeably higher in the United States, so many changed their plans, sent for their families, and settled in the New World. Getting here was not easy, but their dreams spurred them on. In *Poland the Knight Among Nations*, published in 1907, Louis E. Van Norman wrote:

> While in Zbaráz I visited a school for peasant children. Its sessions were held in a rustic little one-room building with the conventional thatched roof. . . . For my especial benefit, the prize scholar was asked where was America. He hesitated a moment, then he said he did not know, except that it was the country to which good Polish boys went when they died.

While life here was an improvement over Poland, it was still difficult. Unskilled Polish laborers had no choice but to begin at the lowest levels of the industrial workforce, working long hours in mills and mines in order to eke out a living. Nonetheless, Polish families and communities worked together to achieve a better life, often adapting survival strategies they had developed as serfs and peasants in Poland to their new surroundings.

A Polish family rests on their porch in Mauch Chunk, Pennsylvania, in this 1940 photograph. Many Poles and other eastern Europeans found work in the American steel and mining industries.

From Poland to Polonia

In America, the hardworking Poles have come a long way. Individual Poles excel in the mainstream of American life—from politics to poetry, theater, film, music, and sports. And as a group, Polish Americans have gained considerable clout, a fact acknowledged by the nation's leaders. As former president Gerald Ford once remarked:

> It has been the policy of mine—and the policy of my Administration—to listen carefully to the voice of Polish America. When it comes to sacrifice and achievement, you have given more, far more than your share in making this the greatest country in the history of mankind.

Hundreds of thousands of Poles left tiny villages in the countryside and resettled in the crowded and confusing streets of New York City, Chicago, and other cities and towns in America. Leaving home was an act of faith, but as more immigrants sought prosperous shores across the Atlantic, Polish villages began to be dominated by the elderly, the ailing, and the young. It was hard for those who left, harder perhaps for those who stayed. But Polish immigrants in America did not forget, and what they saw as a moral obligation propelled them to keep up contacts with relatives and friends still in Poland and also with others who had made the long journey and had scattered across 3,000 miles of America. Because so many of the immigrants

In 1974, parishioners of St. Valentine's Polish National Catholic Church receive Communion in Northampton, Massachusetts.

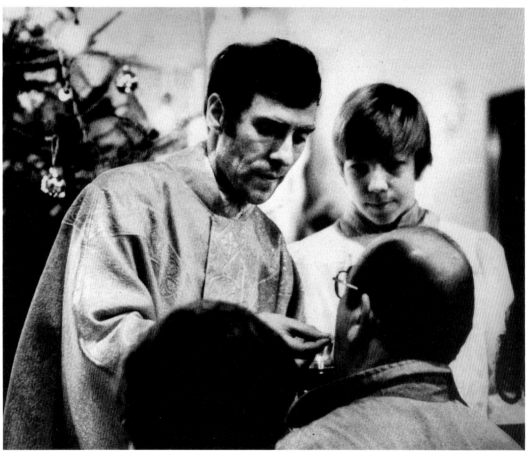

had similar backgrounds and experiences in the New World they felt encouraged to band together to ease the ordeal of readjustment. The large network of Polish Americans led one Greek immigrant to remark:

> We have been in America for six months . . . We have neither heard English nor become acquainted with Americans. In the mill there worked Polish men and women and only Polish was spoken in the factory and in the streets of the small town.

A Greek friend added, "I believe the captain of our ship made a mistake and instead of bringing us to America brought us to Poland." ✎

CRACOVIA.

RVDAVA FLVVIVS

THE PEOPLE OF THE FIELDS

Poland is a nation in eastern Europe, bordered on the west by Germany; on the south by the Czech Republic; on the east by the Ukraine and other republics of the former Soviet Union; and on the north by Lithuania and the Baltic Sea. It measures approximately 121,000 square miles, which makes it roughly the size of the state of New Mexico. Today, largely because of the destruction visited upon it during World War II, its population of approximately 37 million is remarkably homogenous: 98 percent are ethnic Poles; 94 percent are Roman Catholics.

This was not always the case. In the centuries before recorded Polish history, the vast Polish plain (which begins east of the Oder River, constitutes two-thirds of Poland's total area, and merges with the Russian steppes) was inhabited at different times by a host of different peoples—Balts, Celts, various Germanic tribes, Mongols, Huns, Scythians, and assorted Slavonic peoples. Many of these were peoples from the east moving westward into Europe, but in the early Middle Ages eastward migrations brought Germans, Dutch, Jews, and Czechs to Poland.

A Mythical Beginning

Poles traditionally trace the origin of their nation to Piast, a peasant boy who according to legend was told by two tall strangers that he would someday rule his land. The earliest Polish royal dynasty is therefore known as the Piast dynasty; it ruled for approximately 500 years and

The bronze doors of Gniezno Cathedral, carved during the 12th century, depict St. Adalbert baptizing converts to Catholicism.

ultimately united the Slavonic tribes that lived on or near the Polish plain into a Polish kingdom. Little is known about Piast as a historical individual; if he did exist, he was most likely a 9th- or 10th-century chieftain of a small Slavonic tribe known as the *Polanie,* or people of the open fields, who lived on the banks of the Warta River near the present-day city of Poznan. Their domain was known as *Polska,* which is how Poles refer to their nation.

The first Piast ruler about whom much is known is Mieszko I, who from about 960 to 992 ruled over a territory stretching from the Oder to the Vistula rivers. He married a Bohemian princess and in 966 was baptized as a Christian. Both his conversion and his marriage were intended to strengthen Mieszko's ties with the Christian kingdom of Bohemia as a bulwark against Germanic expansion from the west. His son Boleslaw I expanded

Poland's boundaries as far east as the Dnieper River and the Carpathian Mountains. But Boleslaw's immediate successors were less successful in protecting the kingdom, and in 1138, when Boleslaw III died, Poland was divided among his five sons. The result was a 182-year era of political fragmentation, characterized by constant fighting among the Piast dukes for control of the capital city of Cracow and for central authority. During this period, Poland suffered frequent depredations at the hands of a number of outside invaders, most notably the Mongols, Lithuanians, and Prussians. The Teutonic Knights, a warring order of monks who had initially been asked by Duke Conrad of Mazovia to assist him in his struggles with the Lithuanians, carved out a sizable independent state along the Baltic Sea in the 13th century.

The period of fragmentation ended with the coronation in 1320 of Wladyslaw I, known as the Short or the Elbow-high. His son, Kazimierz III (also called Kazimierz the Great), took the throne in 1333. Kazimierz greatly contributed to Poland's unification: he improved Poland's national defense, instituted far-reaching administrative reforms, introduced a new silver currency, and in 1364 established the first Polish university, the Cracovian Academy (later known as the Jagiellonian University).

Kazimierz also encouraged Jewish settlement in Poland. Jews, who were frequently persecuted throughout Europe because they did not practice the dominant Christianity, readily moved to the more tolerant Poland, which in time became home to the largest Jewish community in the world. But while Jews enjoyed far greater freedom (including the protection of person, property, and the practice of religion) in Poland than they did elsewhere in Europe, they did not enjoy the same liberties as Polish Christians. Their right to own land was restricted; they were forbidden to enter certain professions; and they were routinely segregated into their own neighborhoods.

Conrad von Thuringen, grand master of the Teutonic Knights, is portrayed in a 13th-century tomb relief.

During the 14th century Poland's King Kazimierz III was widely known as a benevolent monarch.

Because of such discrimination, as well as differences in religion, Polish-Jewish culture differed significantly from Polish-Christian culture, and when Polish Jews came to the United States they did not settle in the same communities as Polish Christians. In addition, anti-Semitic feeling in Poland sometimes flared into violence and murder; not surprisingly, such incidents prompted many Jews to emigrate. Since it is so distinct, the history of Polish-Jewish immigration into the United States is not dealt with in this book; for greater discussion of the Polish-Jewish immigrants, see another book in this series entitled *The Jewish Americans*.

Nic o nas bez nas

Kazimierz the Great died childless and bequeathed his kingdom to his nephew Louis I, king of Hungary. In order to retain the loyalty and support of Poland's nobles, who were already demonstrating the independence for which they would become famous, Louis was forced to grant them several important concessions. The most notable of these was embodied in the 1374 Statute of Kosice, which provided that the nobility could not be taxed above a certain amount without its consent. This represented an important check on the power of the king at a time when the prevailing practice in much of Europe was to grant the monarch absolute power. In exchange, the nobles agreed to recognize Louis's daughter Jadwiga as ruler after his death.

Jadwiga took the throne in 1384; two years later she wed Jagiello, grand duke of Lithuania. Their wedding united two of the most dynamic kingdoms of central and eastern Europe. Jadwiga died childless in 1399; Jagiello, who ruled Poland as Wladyslaw II, accepted Roman Catholicism (Lithuania had until this time been the last pagan nation in Europe) and expanded Poland's borders, especially by defeating the Teutonic Knights in

The Sejm, Poland's parliament, granted exceptional power to individual noblemen.

1410 at the Battle of Grunwald. Wladyslaw II's direct descendants from his later marriages, known as the Jagiellonian monarchs, ruled Poland for the next 187 years.

Wladyslaw II's son Kazimierz IV took the throne in 1447 and ruled for 45 years, becoming known as the Father of Europe. His children included three queens, four kings, a saint, and a cardinal, but Kazimierz IV and his descendants were destined to see their power wane in comparison with that of the increasingly assertive Polish nobility. In 1454, at Nieszawa, Kazimierz IV conceded to the nobility that no new tax would be levied nor an army raised without their consent—remarkable privileges that some historians consider the Polish equivalent of England's Magna Carta.

Perhaps the most critical circumstance in determining Poland's modern history has been its location between Germany and Russia. The decline of the Teutonic Knights temporarily removed one menace from Poland's western borders, but the consolidation and expansion of Muscovy, which would eventually become the modern state of Russia, threatened the Jagiellonian monarchs with a potential danger to the east. Mindful of the need for increased vigilance, Poland's kings found it necessary to provide the nobility with greater power in exchange for the military assistance necessary to secure the nation's frontiers. In 1505, the nobles forced King Alexander to accept the Nihil Novi statute, which established the primacy of the lower chamber of parliament (Sejm) over the senate and ruled that no new laws could be introduced without the consent of both chambers. This power gave the nobility, represented in the parliament's lower house, the means to steadily increase its strength, chiefly by withholding its approval on measures the crown deemed essential until the king granted it new privileges. The slogan *Nic o nas bez nas* ("Nothing about us without us") embodied the nobles' attitude toward governance.

The 16th century is often called Poland's *Zloty Wiek*, or "golden age." It was one of the largest and most pow-

During the 16th century Nicolaus Copernicus pioneered the science of modern astronomy.

erful nations in Europe. During a time when most of Europe was convulsed in religious warfare between Roman Catholics and Protestants, Poland was comparatively a bastion of tolerance, home to Roman Catholics, Lutherans and members of other Protestant sects, Jews, Orthodox Catholics, and Muslims. Indeed, in 1573, a Statute of General Toleration was passed, and Poland became known as the "land without stakes," meaning that religious and other dissenters did not have to fear official persecution there. Poland's scientists, poets, and politicians made Cracow a center of Renaissance learning. The astronomer Nicolaus Copernicus revolutionized humankind's conception of its place in the universe by demonstrating that the earth revolved around the sun. The poet Jan Kochanowski is often credited with founding Poland's rich literary tradition; before him, literary and scholarly work was usually written in Latin, not Polish.

Kochanowski's contemporary, Jan Zamoyski, did much to build a Polish theory of government called noble democracy. Noble democracy in many ways anticipated the ideals of the English, American, and French revolutions of the 17th and 18th centuries, especially in its emphasis on the right of those affected by legislation (particularly taxation) to be represented in government and its willingness to limit the power of the king. But the

A political cartoon from 1774 satirizes the first partition of Poland, the "plumcake," by greedy European monarchs.

term noble democracy did not mean an especially virtuous form of democracy; it meant democracy for the nobility—and the nobility alone. Indeed, during the very time that Poland's nobility was gaining rights, Poland's peasantry (the vast majority of its population) was losing rights and being reduced to serfdom. Unlike independent peasants, serfs were required by law to work for a lord on his land and could not change profession, marry, or move without their lord's permission.

Noble ascendancy reached its apogee in 1569 with the Union of Lublin, which prepared for the impending demise of the Jagiellonian dynasty and the creation of a new political entity known as the *Respublica*—the Polish-Lithuanian Commonwealth. The treaty formalized a constitutional union between Poland and Lithuania and provided means for its continuance after the death of Zygmunt August, the last of the Jagiellonians. Both Poland and Lithuania were to keep their separate laws and institutions, but the two countries would be jointly governed by an elected king and a common Sejm. After the death of Zygmunt August in 1572, Zamoyski provided additional refinements. Kings would henceforth be elected by the mounted assembly of the entire nobility; they would not be crowned until they swore a solemn oath to uphold the policy of toleration, the practice of royal elections, the regular assembly of the Sejm, the privileges of the nobility, the review of royal policy by 16 senators in permanent residence at the royal court, and the nobility's right to approve all taxes, declarations of war, and foreign treaties. Moreover, the nobility reserved for itself the right of resistance—the privilege and duty to overthrow an unjust ruler, by use of armed force if necessary.

The death of King Zygmunt August, last of the Jagiellonians, led to the union of Poland and Lithuania into the Respublica.

The Respublica

Poland was now a constitutional monarchy. The nobility was justifiably proud of the degree of independence and influence it had attained—but Poland would find it difficult to maintain a balance between freedom from governmental authority and the necessary exercise of governmental power. The 11 kings who were elected during the 223 years of the Respublica's existence were, as the historian Norman Davies has pointed out, a "random selection of talent, mediocrity, and nonentity," but they all would have had to have been exceptional for Poland to have resolved the contradictions that troubled it. The Polish nobles, who at 10 percent of the country's population constituted the largest European nobility, believed that they lived in an exceptionally free and democratic country. Compared to many other European nations at the time, Poland did enjoy an enviable degree of democracy, but it was a gentry democracy in which political rights and privileges and the ideals of independence and equality were limited to the members of only one class.

The nobility's monopoly on power meant that it could single-mindedly pursue its own interests to the detriment of the rest of the country, particularly after the institution of the *liberum veto* in 1652. The liberum veto required the unanimous consent of the Sejm for the passage of any measure; accordingly, it also meant that any one member could kill any legislation and even dissolve the Sejm in pursuit of his own personal interests. The liberum veto arose out of the Polish nobility's belief that government should govern only by the consent of the governed and the "conviction," in Davies's words, "that any good law must have the consent of all those whose duty it is to enforce it," but it led to deadlock and paralysis. By the reign of August III, which began in 1733, only one diet (legislature), in a span of 30 years, succeeded in passing any legislation at all. It is not surprising that nobles opposed to reform boasted: *"Polska nierzadem stoi!"* (Poland survives through anarchy!)

External pressure combined with internal tension to further weaken Poland, which was forced to fight off incursions from Russia, Sweden, and Turkey in the 17th century, with an accompanying loss of territory. Poland also had to concern itself with internal dissent in the form of nobles, such as Prince Jerzy Lubomirski, exercising their right of resistance through rebellion, and revolts by subject peoples, such as the Ukrainian Cossacks. Throughout this period, large segments of Polish society, especially the serfs, grew increasingly impoverished. In the meantime, Poland's immediate neighbors—Russia, Prussia, and Austria—were gaining strength, with Russia, especially, able to exert a growing influence over Poland's affairs.

Dissolution

Poland was in dire need of drastic internal reform, but its neighbors, particularly Russia, which now regarded Poland as a compliant buffer state, consistently stymied any attempts at revitalization. Stanislaw II Augustus Poniatowski, the last Polish king, was elected in 1764 with Russian support, but he nevertheless attempted to implement badly needed changes, including the abolition of the liberum veto. Russia responded by joining with Austria and Prussia to partition Poland; each nation simply carved off a chunk of Poland along its own borders. These helpings satisfied Poland's neighbors for a short while, but after the so-called Great Sejm adopted a new constitution in 1791 that abolished the liberum veto, Russia again grew hungry. It seized most of Lithuania and the Ukraine, while Prussia took a sizable portion of western Poland. Led by Poniatowski and American revolutionary war hero Tadeusz Kościuszko, the Poles resisted, but they were quickly crushed. In January 1793, the Sejm was forced to proclaim the second partition and the abolition of the constitution. What remained of the nominally independent Poland was little more than a Russian puppet state. Despite a national uprising led by Kościuszko in 1794, it was divided among Russia, Prussia, and Austria the following year. Poland had disappeared from the map of Europe. ∾

Two Polish peasants view their livestock on a farm near the Russian border in 1924.

REASONS TO LEAVE

Not surprisingly, the Polish nobility was generally opposed to the partitions, since under Russian, Prussian, or Austrian rule they lost most of their liberties and power. Beginning in the 1760s many of these Poles left or were forced to leave the area, and large communities of exiles formed in various foreign cities, particularly Paris, where they agitated for the restoration of Poland. The more radical of these nobles also committed themselves to fostering the ideals of democracy and the right of people to govern themselves around the world. These idealistic aristocrats found a likely cause when a group of colonists in North America began a rebellion to throw off British rule.

The Spirit of '76

The colonists' fight for their independence did indeed produce "a shot heard around the world," which attracted a substantial number of Polish adventurers, radicals, and revolutionaries—few of whom intended to settle permanently in North America. Among those who arrived during this period, two became heroes still revered by Polish Americans, and throughout the United States their names grace monuments and bridges and appear on the mastheads of fraternal organizations and businesses.

One such revolutionary who fought for freedom both in the United States and Poland was Tadeusz Kościuszko, born in 1746. After attending military schools in Warsaw and Paris, Kościuszko offered his services to the American revolutionaries. He served with distinction and was responsible for the fortifications at the Battle of Saratoga, the turning point of the war. In 1783 he returned to Poland and became involved with efforts to reform Poland's government by drawing up a constitution along the lines of the one ratified in the United States in 1789. The Polish constitution, ratified in 1791, was different from the American one (it preserved both the monarchy and serfdom, for example), but it did expand the rights of the nobility to Poland's growing middle class, and it provided for the liberation of any serf from another country that fled into Poland. This last provision was considered too provocative by the Russians, who invaded Poland (defeating Kościuszko's forces in the process) and instigated the partition of 1793.

The next year Kościuszko led a national rebellion against Russia and Prussia. The effort failed and Kościuszko, after a brief term of imprisonment, went back to the United States, serving as liaison between Thomas Jefferson and the leaders of revolutionary France. Just as Kościuszko had championed the rights of serfs in Poland, he advocated the rights of slaves in the United States, requesting in his last will and testament—dated May 5, 1789—that Jefferson sell off his property and use the profits to free slaves:

> I, Thaddeus Kościuszko, being just in my departure from America do hereby declare and direct that should I make no other testamentary disposition of my property in the United States, I hereby authorize my friend Thomas Jefferson to employ the whole thereof in purchasing Negroes from among his own or any other and giving them liberty in my name, in giving them an education in trade or otherwise and in having them instructed for their new condition in the duties of morality which may make them good neighbors, good fathers or mothers, husbands, or wives, and in their duties as citizens teaching them to be defenders of the

Count Kazimierz Pulaski fought valiantly for the colonial forces in the revolutionary war.

Tadeusz Kosciuszko attained the rank of general in the Polish army.

Liberty and Country and of the good order of society and in whatsoever may make them happy and useful.

Kościuszko died in 1817. Unfortunately, because of Virginia's laws, his humanitarian bequest was never fulfilled.

Another Polish-American hero, Count Kazimierz Pulaski, born in 1747, belonged to a noble family in Poland. In 1768 he and his father formed a confederation that sought to free Poland of Russian influence by rebelling against King Stanislaw II, whom they saw as a pawn of Moscow. Russian troops quashed the confederation's troops in 1772, and the younger Pulaski fled to Turkey,

An engraving by F. Girsch shows George Washington with the foreign officers who fought in the revolutionary war.

Prussia, and eventually France, where he met Benjamin Franklin, who was in Paris on a diplomatic mission to drum up support for the American Revolution. Franklin gave Pulaski a letter of introduction to George Washington, and the Pole set off across the Atlantic in 1777. Joining the colonial forces, he organized his own cavalry command and fought valiantly until the British attack on Savannah, Georgia, where he was mortally wounded in October 1779.

The First Wave

While a few Poles had settled in America in colonial times, the arrival of Kościuszko and Pulaski marked the beginning of a wave of Polish political immigration that lasted until about 1870. These immigrants, who were relatively few in number and were mostly from the upper classes, left Poland because of political conditions in their partitioned homeland. In the mid-1810s, the section of Poland ruled by Russia was granted a small measure of autonomy, but conflicts continued between the Polish nobles, who wanted greater independence, and the Russian czar, who wished to keep control of the country. In 1830, Poles rebelled against the rule of Russian czar Nicholas I in an uprising known as the November Insurrection. Russian troops marched into Warsaw and put down the revolt, destroying any hope of Polish independence. About 400 Poles escaped to the United States. After another uprising in 1863, when the czar instituted a Russification policy to make the Polish people adopt Russian culture and language, Poles fled to European capitals such as Geneva, Paris, and London, and American metropolises such as New York, Chicago, and San Francisco.

The Polish struggle for independence inspired Americans who believed that they shared with the Poles the same democratic and republican ideals and who remembered the contributions made by Kościuszko and Pulaski to America's freedom. The Polish American

Sir Casimir S. Gzowski, an insurrectionist in the Polish uprising of 1830, later immigrated to North America, where he helped develop the Canadian railroad and also assisted in building the International Bridge, which spans the Niagara River.

Committee in Paris raised a large sum for the Polish rebels, soliciting the funds through an appeal drafted by the American novelist James Fenimore Cooper. Cooper's passionate interest in helping Poland began in 1830, when he met the Polish poet Adam Mickiewicz in Rome. Mickiewicz also greatly impressed the American inventor Samuel F. B. Morse, and he too joined the cause. After the November 1830 insurrection, political exiles conceived the idea of setting up a new Poland in America. They summoned their compatriots with these words:

> Poles! Let us leave that wretched country now no more our own though soaked with the blood of her best defenders. . . . America is the only country worthy of affording an asylum to men who have sacrificed everything for freedom. There Poland will be enshrined in our hearts, and Heaven will perhaps bless our devotion.

Sizable groups of Polish immigrants answered the call as early as 1834, but the communities they established did not always succeed. For example, on December 21, 1849, the sailing ship *Manchester* departed from Le Havre, France, for a long and wearisome voyage to New Orleans, Louisiana. The ship's passengers included 105 men, women, and children who had formed the first community of Polish immigrants living in France as a consequence of the November uprising. The immigrants' leader, a 54-year-old doctor named Francis Lawrynowicz, planned to set up a colony of adjacent farms in Louisiana. But shortly after the group arrived there, yellow fever blanketed the state and killed thousands, among them the settlers led by Dr. Lawrynowicz.

Another 15 years would pass before the first permanent Polish settlement in the United States was founded. In 1854 Father Leopold Moczygemba and a group of about 100 families established in Texas the town of Panna Maria (Polish for the Virgin Mary). The colonists

Father Leopold Moczygemba, the Franciscan friar who helped found Panna Maria, Texas, the first Polish-American settlement.

built a church and a school, where the organist taught the three Rs (in Polish), the pastor taught religion, and a native-born American instructed the children in the English language and sewing. Panna Maria was in many ways a harbinger of things to come. The settlers were mostly peasants, and they came to Texas more because of the available farmland than because of the oppressive political climate in Poland. They would be followed by a flood of Polish immigrants seeking greater economic opportunities in the New World.

The Next Wave

The late 19th century saw a tremendous influx of Polish immigrants into the United States—one that easily dwarfed the previous immigration. Accurate immigration figures are difficult to find—due to the partitions, many Poles were listed in immigration records as being Russian, Prussian, or Austrian—but in 1870 the Polish population in the United States was probably less than 30,000. By 1900, Polish Americans numbered in the hundreds of thousands, and a few decades later they would number in the millions.

Reasons to Leave

The factors that led to this tremendous increase in immigration were many and complex. One reason was that the United States government encouraged foreigners to come to America, especially after the Civil War depleted the nation's economic and cultural resources. In his Fourth Annual Message in 1864, President Abraham Lincoln said, "I regard our immigrants as one of the principal replenishing streams which are appointed by providence to repair the ravages of internal war and its waste of national strength and health." Private businesses and industries in the United States also encouraged much-needed laborers to emigrate, sending agents to Europe to recruit workers.

But events in partitioned Poland were just as important, if not more so. By the late 1860s, the Russian, Prussian, and Austrian rulers of Poland had abolished serfdom. Polish peasants could now hold their own land and change their place of residence at will. As wealthier or luckier peasants purchased larger and larger plots of land, poorer peasants were left with an inadequate amount of land to support their families or, worst of all, no land whatsoever. (In Prussia this process was hastened by the government's policy of buying Polish land and turning it over to German settlers in an attempt to Germanize the area.)

Peasants soon discovered that they could supplement their incomes by sending a family member (usually a son or husband) to the more industrial parts of Europe to work as a laborer. There, wages were relatively high, and a laborer who lived simply could save enough money in a few years to buy his family livestock or land when he returned to his village. Even wealthier peasant families realized that having a relative or two working in a foreign factory or mine was a lucrative proposition, and the practice became widely popular. Historians estimate that from 1860 to 1914, some 9 million Poles migrated temporarily or permanently, most of them in search of work.

Not surprisingly, many of these laborers traveled to the United States, where wages were higher than in Europe. Sometimes called *za chlebem*—or "for-bread" immigrants—these people did not plan to settle permanently in America. They hoped they could save enough money to return to Poland and build a better life. In the words of one young immigrant, a 26-year-old Polish Catholic:

> I intend to go in a few days to a Jewish agent in Konstnaty- now to make an arrangement for crossing the frontier with- out a passport, for I am absolutely determined to go now to New York or Philadelphia to earn some hundreds of roubles there within 2 or 3 years then to come back to our country and rent a mill or buy a piece of land with the money collected in this way.

Poles who went to the United States sent letters home that described a land of abundant opportunity and more often than not contained money. Eventually, some returned to their home villages wearing fancy "city" clothing and bought homes and land with the money they had earned abroad.

For those who were struggling simply to survive, it was easy to be impressed by the seeming opulence. One disillusioned Pole, 24 years old and married, wrote:

> I have a very great wish to go to America. I want to leave my native country because we are 6 children and we have very little land, only about 6 morgs [about 13 acres] and some small farm-buildings, so that our whole farm is worth 1200 roubles at the highest. And my parents are still young;

father is 48 and mother 42 years old. So it is difficult for us to live. . . . Here in our country one must work plenty and wages are very small, just enough to live, so I would like to go in the name of our Lord God; perhaps I would earn more there.

Another immigrant echoed these sentiments.

I want to go to America, but I have no means at all because I am poor and having nothing but the ten fingers of my hands, a wife and 9 children. I have no work at all, although I am strong and healthy and only 45 years old, I cannot earn for my family. I have been already in Dabrowa, Sosnowiec, Zawiercie and Lodz, wherever I could go, and nowhere could I earn well. And here the children call for food and clothing and more or less education. I wish to work, not easily only but even hard, but what can I do? I will not go to steal and I have no work.

An Austrian print from the 1870s satirizes emigration agents swindling Polish peasants.

Getting to the United States was not an easy matter. Traveling across the Atlantic was expensive, and few

immigrants arrived with anything more than spare change left over. Most of the Poles who came over at this time traveled in steerage—the crowded holds of American-bound cargo ships. The experience on board often proved more alarming than any hardship awaiting them in the United States. Crammed into filthy quarters, the immigrants fell prey to seasickness, infectious disease, and frequent outbursts of violence. But these conditions did not deter them.

The Lady of the Harbor

In 1899 Poles ranked fourth among the population of new arrivals. The next year, they surpassed the Irish and took third place. At this time, 10 percent of all immigrants were Polish. Between 1870 and 1914, more than 2 million Poles immigrated to the United States.

They joined a massive European tide. From 1855 to 1890, 8 million newcomers landed at Castle Garden, a refurbished military post run by New York State immigration officials, where new arrivals submitted to a battery of examinations. According to an 1882 U.S. law, "any convict, lunatic, idiot, or any person unable to take care of himself or herself without becoming a public charge" could not be allowed into the country, and in the 1890s those "suffering from a loathsome or dangerous contagious disease" were banned as well. Rejects were shipped back home free of charge, but since many would-be immigrants had spent nearly all they had on passage to the United States, being rejected was usually a disaster. With immigrants so eager to be let in, the potential for corruption among administrators was high. Bribery and blackmail became so commonplace that one official described the process as "a perfect farce."

The federal government, dismayed at the state's handling of immigrants, decided to step in and take over. In 1892 the government built a new facility on Ellis Island to process the throngs of foreigners who disembarked in New York Harbor. Corruption was still fairly common until 1901, when President Theodore Roosevelt vigorously purged and reformed the immigration administration. From 1890 to 1930, the Ellis Island station admitted 16 million people into the United States.

Prospective immigrants were interviewed and given medical examinations (a process that took an average of 45 minutes), and the vast majority of them were approved. Indeed, the immigrants had been screened long before they reached the United States, both by the U.S. embassies in their countries of departure that had granted them entry permits and by the shipping companies that had to transport any rejects. Nonetheless, the immigration process was nerve-racking. During the early 1900s, Ellis Island's facilities were routinely overwhelmed by the number of people to be processed, and some immigrants had to wait hours or even overnight to be interviewed and examined. During the wait, anxieties mounted and rumors spread about the sorts of questions that would be asked and the kinds of answers that would result in rejection.

Once an immigrant was approved, he or she was free to enter the country. While some immigrants were met in New York by family or friends who had preceded them, most needed to travel to wherever their people had set-

Hopeful immigrants apply for entry permits at the United States embassy in Warsaw sometime during the 1920s.

At Ellis Island, Polish immigrants in quarantine dance beneath a multilingual sign, informing them that their meals will be free of charge.

tled—a confusing prospect for someone in a new country who did not speak the language. Established Poles formed the Polish Society to help new arrivals find transportation to other cities or obtain housing in New York. By train, ship, or subway these immigrants made their way to new homes, new jobs, and a new life. ∿

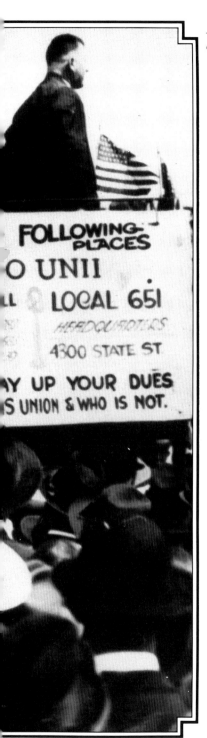

Polish workers rally in Chicago during the mid-20th century.

LIFE IN AMERICA

Polish immigrants had many obstacles to hurdle. Acting individually, the new arrivals might have felt overwhelmed, but by forming communities they managed to help one another out. As one immigrant wrote to his family back home: "I have work, I'm not hungry, only I have not yet laughed since I came to America . . . . But come and see that here no one goes to bed on an empty stomach because one Pole will save another, if he can."

First Steps

Most of the immigrants at the turn of the century were young men, who came singly or in groups. Such an immigrant usually carried only a small amount of money—in the late 19th century the average Polish newcomer brought less than $14. Some of the luckier travelers also had a piece of paper with the address of a relative or friend written on it. Sometimes, however, the location was transcribed so poorly from Polish to English that native-born Americans were at a loss to guide immigrants to their desired destination. One Polish boy arrived at Ellis Island with an address that read:

Pittsburgh, Pa., Panewna
Stait 16 Babereia 47

After two hours of deciphering, a kind and patient secretary at Pittsburgh's Young Men's Christian Association (YMCA) produced the correct address:

45

Penn Ave., 16 Street
47 Mulberry Alley

In addition to a lack of funds and connections, Polish immigrants nearly always lacked education. While literacy was highly valued by Polish peasants (between two-thirds and three-fourths of turn-of-the-century Polish immigrants could read and write), higher education in Poland was reserved for the gentry, and the vast majority of Poles had no specialized learning or job training.

As a result, Polish laborers had to begin on the lowest rung of the employment ladder. Pennsylvania mining towns, such as Wilkes-Barre and Hazleton, employed unskilled laborers, as did the steel centers of Pittsburgh and Cleveland. Polish immigrants also gravitated to the mills, slaughterhouses, refineries, and foundries of Toledo, Ohio; South Bend, Indiana; Milwaukee, Wisconsin; Minneapolis-St. Paul, Minnesota; Omaha, Nebraska; St. Louis, Missouri; and Chicago, Illinois.

Slaughterhouse workers stir a vat of boiling pigs.

Sausage makers practice their craft at a meat-packing house.

Large Polish communities also sprang up in New York, Buffalo, and Detroit.

For men who had worked outdoors their whole lives, laboring in underground mines or sweltering foundries required difficult adjustments. The hours were often long, the work unpleasant, and the pay low. John J. Bukowszyk's *And My Children Do Not Know Me,* a history of Polish Americans, quotes an anonymous letter sent to the homeland from Brooklyn, New York, bemoaning the conditions that greeted Poles in the New World:

> What people from America write to Poland is all bluster; there is not a word of truth. For in America Poles work like cattle. Where a dog does not want to sit, there the Pole is made to sit, and the poor wretch works because he wants to eat.

In 1931, Robert Unger, the American-born child of Polish and German immigrants, stands atop New York's Empire State Building, which he helped to construct.

Industrial employment at the turn of the century was also far from safe. Many Poles operated heavy machinery that cost them life and limb. A New York Department of Labor survey from 1902-3 listed the following casualties:

Pobish, Michael; helper in print shop, 26 years of age; married; . . . instantly killed on December 21, 1902, while painting runway of electric traveling crane in erecting shop; crane crushing body so badly so as to expose heart to view . . . Walazinovice, Simon; floor helper; 38 years of age; married; . . . fatally injured on April 7, 1903, in the tank shop; while helping unload boiler plate, clamp slipped off plate which was suspended in air by lifting crane, and fell on Walazinovice, badly crushing abdomen and lower portion of body; death resulted almost immediately.

Getting promoted out of such menial and dangerous work was often difficult due to growing anti-immigrant sentiment in the United States. The record numbers of newcomers—many of them from southern and eastern Europe—worried many native-born Americans and earlier immigrant generations who feared for their jobs and the stability of their neighborhoods. American newspapers complained loudly of "the mixed population with

LESLIE'S WEEKLY
McKINLEY EXTRA

Vol. XCIII.—EXTRA NUMBER.   *New York, September 9, 1901*   PRICE 10 CENTS

Leon F. Czolgosz—an American-born anarchist (a person opposed to all forms of government) of Polish descent— peers out from behind prison bars in 1901 after assassinating President William McKinley. Czolgosz's crime shocked the nation, and although he was not an immigrant, his ethnicity and radical politics (which were more popular in eastern Europe than in the United States) convinced many Americans that all Poles were a threat.

which we are afflicted." Anyone who spoke halting or broken English became fair game for ridicule and discrimination. Employers sometimes withheld wages and often denied promotions to newcomers. One mine foreman recalled, "When [the managers] had a list of names for promotions: White, McKinnley, Baumgarten, Borowski, and so on, they tended to scratch out the 'Hunky' [eastern European] ones."

Families and Communities

While life in the United States was far from easy, for many Poles conditions in America were still a decided improvement over those in Poland—jobs were more plentiful, wages were higher, and houses and land were more available. Many immigrants who had planned to return to Poland decided to stay instead; others returned to Poland only to discover that opportunities were better in the United States. The predominantly male immi-

Students gather for a group portrait at the St. Joseph School in Meyersville, Texas.

grants began to send for their families, relations, and close friends. Single men arranged to marry the sisters or cousins of their coworkers, and laborers convinced their employers to hire their brothers and sons.

Supporting an entire family on the salary of a solitary mine or mill worker was all but impossible, so all family members pitched in, much as they had helped with the farmwork in Poland. Sons who were in their teens or older joined their fathers at work, while daughters found jobs as factory workers or domestic servants. Work placed such a strain on every member of the family that education seemed a luxury, hardly important in the daily

Slavic children play on a slag heap, c. 1900.

A 1920 photograph shows the wife of a Slavic miner in Pennsylvania doing the weekly wash.

struggle for survival. Since higher education had been traditionally reserved for the nobility in Poland—and the noble class was often strongly resented by the only recently liberated peasantry—Polish Americans from peasant backgrounds who sought higher education often found themselves ostracized by the larger community, who viewed them as traitors to their class.

Schooling for children seemed necessary only up to the age (usually under 10 years old) when they received their First Communion, which required a modicum of religious instruction. Toward this end, Polish Americans established many Catholic schools in their neighborhoods, schools which often helped keep the group together, physically as well as culturally. Other Polish-American children attended public schools, but with hostility toward immigrants reaching new highs in the 1910s and 1920s, the atmosphere of many such schools was far from encouraging. Many first- and second-generation Polish Americans who attended public schools were teased for their clothes, their accents, and their names—by students and teachers alike. One second-generation Polish-American woman who dropped out of elementary school recalled, "We felt inferior. I quit because I was embarrassed, always embarrassed about

Immigrants from eastern Europe often lived in squalid tenement buildings.

Milwaukee's "Little Poland" was one of many Polish neighborhoods that sprang up across the Midwest during the 1800s.

everything and myself. Many of our [people] quit school early because we were all sort of scared." Consequently, during the early 20th century Polish Americans were one of the least-educated ethnic groups in the country.

Married women also worked, but usually not outside the home. Instead, they contributed to their family's income by growing food and raising livestock in their backyards, running laundry or dressmaking businesses from their homes, and taking in boarders, generally Polish men who had immigrated more recently. The practice of taking in boarders—called *trzymanie bortnikow*—became an important feature of Polish-American life in the early 1900s. Room and board cost from two to three dollars per month, and the boarders often interacted like a family. The houses themselves resembled Old World residences, with pigs, goats, chickens, and cows roaming the backyards, much to the dismay of neighbors. Boardinghouses were usually located near the places where the men found work—in coal or steel mines or in factories in the poorer sections of towns and cities.

Often men who boarded together worked together, and many originally came from the same village or region in Poland. Many towns in the Midwest and parts of the Northeast developed close-knit Polish-American communities that became self-supporting. As their population grew, an increasing number of Poles congregated in

A group of Polish Americans attend class in order to prepare for the U.S. citizenship examination.

central areas, bringing a wide variety of useful skills. Shoemakers, dressmakers, butchers, and bakers set up shops that served the ethnic community and further bound its members together.

Priest-Titans

The local parish invariably served as the focal point of the community, just as it had in Poland. It catered to religious needs and also provided a social center where immigrants could meet and converse about life in the New World. When immigrants faced poverty or eviction or simply needed comfort, they often turned to the men who presided over the parishes—the priests. So powerful and influential did these clerics become that they were referred to as priest-titans. As the embodiment of traditions cherished by Poles since the Middle Ages, the church helped ease the immigrants' transition to their new world.

Polish Catholics brought to North America a number of distinctive practices from the Old World. Although they shared with their coreligionists a devout veneration of the Virgin (whom the Poles referred to as Mary, Queen of Poland), Poles revered their own saints,

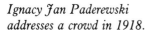

Ignacy Jan Paderewski addresses a crowd in 1918.

spoke Polish during religious ceremonies, and celebrated certain rites in a traditional way that kept alive a heritage that traced back nearly 1,000 years. In Europe, the church had played a major role in defending Polish culture against the Russification and Germanization efforts of the Russian and Prussian empires; in North America, Poles built over 950 of their own Roman Catholic and Polish National Catholic churches and labored to preserve the "Polishness" of these parishes. As one Polish American characterized the situation, "Without the Church we have lost our identity."

This attitude led to conflicts with the Irish Catholics who monopolized the Roman Catholic church in America in the late 19th and early 20th centuries. While Irish bishops engaged in power struggles with members of nearly all other Catholic immigrant groups, their policy of Americanizing the church—making English the language spoken in confession and other church events outside of the Latin mass, for example—was especially repellent to Polish Catholics. Eventually, Poles set up their own Polish-language churches, both within and (in the case of the Polish National Catholic church) outside of the Roman Catholic church.

Fraternal Organizations

The need for fellowship and assistance led in turn to mutual aid societies that immigrants could appeal to in emergencies. Over time, these evolved into cultural and political groups as well as insurance organizations. Such Polish-American fraternal organizations have succeeded in providing economic assistance to immigrants and their families, lobbying for political goals, and maintaining Polish culture in America. Founded in 1880, the Polish National Alliance (PNA) emphasized the restoration of Poland's independence and the use of the vote by Polish immigrants to further that goal. In contrast, the Polish Roman Catholic Union (PRCU), founded in 1873, discouraged Americanization in any form. Despite their differing outlooks, these two frater-

Initially a socialist, Marshal Józéf Pilsudski ended his career as a right-wing dictator, backed by the Polish military.

nals, along with many others, contributed to a heightened sense of patriotism within the Polish-American community.

Another group, the Polish Women's Alliance, an expression of immigrant nationalism and feminism, worked toward the restoration of Poland as a part of the agenda of the international peace movement. In the calm before the First World War they proclaimed:

> Poland today is like Lazarus, thrown on the bed of blood, fire and embers—murdering her own children by order of her enemies—sinking the steel in the breasts of her own sons, fathers and brothers. . . . In view of this terrible tax of blood, property and life devoured by war from our own unhappy nation, which is a crime of humanity and the world—we, the daughters of this downtrodden and blood bespattered unhappy country, do raise our mighty voice of mothers, daughters, sisters and wives suffering beyond measure, calling to all nations.

Strength in numbers was combined with a passionate belief in their cause. After nearly a decade of lobbying, in 1910, monuments to Polish heroes Pulaski and Kościuszko were unveiled in the nation's capital on the 500th anniversary of the Battle of Grunwald, in which Poland defeated the Teutonic Knights.

Restoration

The 1910s saw a resurgence of interest in Poland by Polish Americans. Indeed, Polish Americans often referred to their settlements in America as the "fourth province of Poland"—the other three being the Polish areas under Russian, German, and Austrian control. As was true of many other subjugated European nationalities, Poles regarded the outbreak of World War I in 1914 as an opportunity to regain their national freedom, especially once U.S. president Woodrow Wilson declared support of the restoration of Poland. World-renowned Polish concert pianist Ignacy Jan Paderewski toured the United

States, raising money for the Polish cause. Polish Americans responded enthusiastically by donating some $20 million to support Polish independence (as well as buying $67 million worth of Liberty Bonds to support the U.S. war effort). In addition, 28,000 Polish-American volunteers joined a specially formed Polish army.

By 1918, Germany stood on the verge of defeat, Russia had withdrawn from the conflict because of revolution and civil war, and Austria had disintegrated. Poland reestablished itself as an independent nation, with Paderewski as prime minister and Józef Pilsudski as head of state and commander of the military. A new Sejm was convened, and in March 1921, Poland implemented one of the most democratic constitutions in all of Europe.

Despite its long history, Poland was not spared the growing pains that often follow a birth (or in this case a rebirth) of independence. World War I's bloody eastern front had been located on Polish territory; millions of Poles had been conscripted to fight in the armies of Russia, Austria, or Germany. At war's end, almost 5 million Poles, out of a total population of 30 million, had died, either on the battlefield or from starvation or disease. Millions more were homeless or displaced; the economy was a wreck. Faced with such an overwhelming job of reconstruction, Poland's fledgling democracy often found itself divided or lacking the resources to carry out the necessary work. By 1926, Pilsudski had seized the reins of power as a dictator, a role he did not relinquish until his death in 1935.

Events in Poland seriously disappointed many Polish Americans, who had hoped that independence would help solve the country's many social problems. Continued requests for aid and the political lobbying of U.S. officials by the Polish government started to wear on many American Poles, who began to turn away from Poland and focus on problems facing Polonia. This trend was encouraged by the U.S. government, which in 1921 passed a new immigration act establishing quotas

German troops invade Poland in 1939.

that severely limited the number of immigrants from eastern and southern Europe (including Poland) allowed into the country.

As the first generation of Polish-American immigrants aged, members of the second and third generations came into their own. Although many of these people spoke Polish as a first language and were very attached to Polish culture, they were more familiar with American culture, making them better able to capitalize on the opportunities America offered. Polish-American industrial workers began to join labor unions in large numbers and to successfully agitate for better pay and work conditions. Although many Poles were still under-educated and shut out of professional fields, they obtained the job training needed to work as skilled laborers or in supervisory positions. Most second-generation parents encouraged their children to stay in school longer.

World War II and Its Aftermath

The attention of Polonia and of the world returned to Poland in September 1939, when Germany, which had been revitalized and rearmed under fascist dictator Adolph Hitler, invaded its eastern neighbor, sparking World War II. Poland's resistance was fierce but no match for the Nazi blitzkrieg, nor for the Soviet attack from the rear a mere two weeks later. (The Soviet attack was part of an agreement between Hitler and Joseph Stalin, dictator of the Soviet Union. The pact quickly fell apart when Germany invaded the Soviet Union in 1941.) No nation suffered more from Nazi depredations than Poland: more than 6 million Poles—18 percent of the population—were killed during the war. Half of these were Polish Jews; the machinery of the Holocaust operated nowhere more efficiently than in Poland, where the largest of Europe's Jewish communities was all but completely exterminated.

Tragedy followed tragedy. The Soviet troops who drove the German forces from Poland in 1945 were hailed as liberators, but they proved to be conquerors when Stalin reneged on his pledge to hold free elections in Poland and instead established a Communist government, manned by Communist Poles beholden to the Soviet Union. Poland was again officially independent, but in reality it was one of the numerous satellite states shackled to the Soviet Union through economic dependence and the calculated, brutal use of political repression and military force. The new Polish government forbade its citizens to emigrate or even travel out of the country, a policy it followed until 1956.

Bombings, warfare, and Nazi and Soviet relocation programs displaced an estimated 12 million Poles from their homes during World War II. Many of those who left or were forced out of Poland during the war refused to return while their nation was under Communist rule.

In the 1940s and 1950s, the U.S. government passed a number of special acts to allow these refugees, called displaced persons, into the country.

These political refugees had generally received a much better education in their homeland than had turn-of-the-century Polish immigrants because the independent Polish government had vastly expanded the nation's schools. Although the more established Polish

During World War II, a group of Polish Americans carry a banner announcing, "Farewell America. We go to fight a despotic emperor for your freedom and ours."

Americans initially distrusted these genteel newcomers, they eventually revitalized Polonia. Both the Nazis and the Soviets targeted intellectuals for persecution, so disproportionate numbers of displaced persons were college professors, writers, and other educators. When they realized that many people in America's Polonia knew next to nothing about Polish history and high culture (subjects that had received little emphasis either in American schools or in the average peasant's education), they organized lectures and published journals, sparking a new interest and pride among American Poles in their heritage. Many refugees joined the Polish American Congress, an organization established in May 1944 as the immigrant community's political voice. In the years since, it has steadfastly demanded the restoration of Poland's independence and worked for the advancement of Americans of Polish origin.

Polish and Proud

After World War II, the number of Polish Americans attending college rose dramatically, and by 1969 almost one-third had advanced beyond high school—one of the highest percentages for any ethnic group. Later generations of Polish Americans embraced the mainstream society of their country and tried to make their own place in it. Some rejected their parents' style of life and moved away from ethnic communities. As one Polish American put it:

> This generation of which I am a part, never had to face the problem of pulling away from Polonia. We had never properly belonged to it. To us it was a slowly decaying world of aged folks living largely in a dream. One day it would pass and there would remain only Americans whose forebears had once been Poles.

But many Polish Americans felt a profound connection to their heritage, supported fraternal organizations, and agitated for the end of Communist rule in Poland.

Corporate executive Edward J. Piszek has struggled to dignify the image of Polish Americans.

The Polish-American community greatly increased its visibility in the 1970s in response to a disturbing trend on the American scene. Beginning in the late 1960s, Polish—or "Polak"—jokes that focused on the lower-class background and peasant heritage of many Poles enjoyed a great vogue. Many television comedians routinely told jokes deprecating Poles, and these jokes gained momentum in the retelling. Books such as *It's Fun to Be a Polak* helped spread the jokes, which reached the highest levels of American society. When Ronald Reagan was running

TRADITION AND FAITH

(Overleaf) During a 1987 trip to the United States, Pope John Paul II visits a Detroit church, addressing its Polish-American congregation in Polish, his native language.

Many Polish Americans continue to honor the traditions and ceremonies of their religious heritage. The baptism rite welcomes a Polish-American infant (above) into the Polish Catholic community in Chicago. (Top right) In accordance with an Easter custom, a priest calls at the home of his parishioners to bless their food on Holy Saturday. (Lower right) Two Polish Americans visit a local church for a moment of private prayer.

Polish Americans have
organized and agitated both to
protect their rights in the United
States and to improve life in
Poland. In Chicago, a Polish-
American woman (top left) signs
a petition circulated to end
martial law in Poland.
Spectators at a parade (lower
left) cheer Illinois state senator
Judy Baar, a Polish American.
(Above) During a Polish festival
in Chicago, a pennant serves to
remind a new generation of the
struggle of Solidarity in Poland.

Polish organizations express their religious, cultural, and political values at festivals such as this one (left) in Chicago. Polish-American communities are dotted with shops, clubs, and mutual aid societies that serve the community as well as perpetuate a sense of unity.

The old and the new: A Polish-American family, its members clothed in both American garb and traditional costumes of the homeland, marches in the annual Pulaski Day parade in New York City.

for president in 1980, he—seemingly without fear of embarrassing or compromising himself in the eyes of voters—told a Polish joke to a crowd of reporters.

Many Polish Americans strongly resented these "humorous" slights, which they felt ignored the considerable economic and educational advances Poles had made in this country and fostered the stereotype that all Poles were crude, poorly educated, and fundamentally stupid. Besides being unflattering, the stereotype had been used in the 1910s and 1920s as a rationale for denying Poles both job promotions and entrance into the United States. To combat these attacks, in 1973 Edward J. Piszek, president of frozen-food manufacturer Mrs. Paul's Kitchens, launched a massive advertising campaign to stamp out Polish jokes. Working with the Orchard Lake schools of Michigan, "Project Pole" was a half-million-dollar affair. It featured literate and intelligent ads, such as the one that showed a picture of celebrated novelist Joseph Conrad (1857–1924, neé Józef Korzeniowski) and read: "One of the greatest storytellers in the English language was a Pole. He changed his name, his language and the course of English literature."

Other Poles followed Piszek's lead. A lawsuit brought against the American Broadcasting Company (ABC) by the Polish American Congress charged the network with refusing to allow equal airtime for a response to jokes viewed by many as "personal attacks on the character, intelligence, hygiene, or appearance" of Americans of Polish descent. And Polish Americans took exception to an insulting skit on the "Carol Burnett Show," sending in bags of critical mail and forcing an apology on the air.

The question of stereotypes still causes controversy in the Polish-American community, especially when it is implied that Poles themselves seem to accept or lend credence to the negative characterizations that exist about them. For example, in 1987 Polish-American historian Stanislaus A. Blejwas wrote a lengthy missive that

Henry and Helen Gulczynski, a young Polish-American couple, proudly hold their baby daughter in 1947.

appeared in the *New York Times Book Review*. The letter concerned remarks made by another Polish American, Czeslaw Milosz, one of the leading Polish-language authors of the 20th century who immigrated to the United States in 1960. After laboring in obscurity for many years, Milosz rose to international celebrity in 1980, when he won the Nobel Prize for literature. He quickly became a source of enormous pride to the Polish-American community, which demanded his presence at a host of cultural events. But Milosz objected to acting as a spokesman for a community that he felt had long neglected him. Indeed, the poet told an interviewer that he resented being invited to give public readings before "a lot of Poles, who come to see a famous Pole to lessen their own feeling of inferiority." Milosz went on to criticize the "incredible cultural crudeness" of many Polish Americans, a condition he traces to the "ghetto" mentality the community brought over from the homeland at the turn of the century. These opinions incensed Blejwas, who in his letter to the *Times* explained the feelings of Polish Americans in these words:

> After a decade of Polish jokes in the national media, jokes which even Mr. Milosz disliked, Polish-Americans took satisfaction in the recognition accorded to Mr. Milosz by the Nobel Prize, and we applauded him. . . . Like any other ethnic group [the Polish Americans] . . . have both good and negative points. Furthermore, their diversity and socioeconomic and cultural integration into American society belies crude (there is that word again!) generalizations and stereotyping. . . . What are the . . . roots of the contempt of some Polish intellectuals for their Polish cousins? Is it due to a political culture still heavily encrusted with gentry contempt for those of lower social origin and rank? Is it simply the arrogance that many intellectuals, regardless of their national identity, felt for the masses? Or, in America, is it that sense of "alienation" our culture provokes which causes a writer of Mr. Milosz's obvious stature to stoop to the level of those who indulge themselves in Polish jokes?

The campaign against Polish jokes in the 1970s formed part of a larger revival of awareness of Polish ethnicity; "Polish and Proud" bumper stickers adorned cars, and "Kiss Me I'm Polish" buttons abounded. The polka—a popular Polish dance—found new popularity that has lasted to the present day. The 1970s also saw a more general vogue of the idea of ethnicity, and Polish Americans joined many other ethnic groups in emphasizing that success in mainstream American society did not require a complete denial of the unique traditions and heritage of the homeland. ✎

In 1925, Stephen Mizwa (top row, second from left) founded the Kosciuszko Foundation, an organization promoting cultural exchange between the United States and Poland.

CELEBRITIES AND CONTRIBUTIONS

In recent years, Polish Americans have entered every arena of national life and have done so in numbers and with talent. No recent Polish American has had a more illustrious career in politics than Edmund Muskie. Born in 1914 to Polish immigrants living in Rumford, Maine, Muskie began his career as a lawyer. After serving in the navy during World War II, he won election to the Maine legislature. In 1955 he became the state's first Polish-American governor and also broke an 18-year Republican monopoly on the office. Three years later he achieved another first, becoming the first Polish American to win a seat in the U.S. Senate. He won reelection in 1964, and in 1968 Muskie became the Democratic party's vice-presidential candidate on a ticket headed by Hubert H. Humphrey. The team lost a close contest to Republicans Richard M. Nixon and Spiro T. Agnew. Muskie reclaimed his Senate seat in 1970.

In the next election year, 1972, he emerged as the top contender for the party's presidential nomination, but his campaign ran aground. A year later, when the Watergate scandal beset the Nixon administration, congressional hearings unearthed evidence that Muskie's bid had been sabotaged by operatives working for the

In 1972, U.S. senator Edmund Muskie displays a bumper sticker bearing his original Polish name.

Republican Committee to Reelect the President. In 1979, Muskie resigned his Senate post to accept an emergency appointment as secretary of state, helping to shore up the ailing administration of President Jimmy Carter. Thereafter Muskie retired from politics but resurfaced in 1986, when President Ronald Reagan appointed him to the Tower Commission, a three-man panel of distinguished public servants charged with reviewing the Iran-Contra affair.

Another Polish American also held high office during the Carter administration: National Security Advisor Zbigniew Brzezinski. Born in Poland in 1928, he became disenchanted with the country's Communist regime and immigrated to Canada and then the United States. He taught government at Harvard University and was on the faculty of Columbia University when Carter appointed him to the National Security Council (NSC) in 1976. In that post he often feuded with Secretary of State Cyrus Vance, who advocated a less combative stance toward the Soviet Union. But Brzezinski and Vance worked together to assist Carter during his greatest presidential triumph: the Camp David peace accord signed in 1979 by Israeli premier Menachem Begin and Egyptian president Anwar Sadat. After Carter lost his reelection bid in 1980, Brzezinski joined Georgetown University's Center for Strategic International Studies, advised Republican presidential candidate George Bush during his 1988 campaign, and published a number of books about the collapse of communism in Europe. Brzezinski's high stature in international circles has resulted in an interesting turn of events: a group of Poles suggested that he should return to the country of his birth and run in its upcoming presidential elections, which will be held in the fall of 1995.

Former National Security Adviser Zbigniew Brzezinski is the author of The Soviet Bloc, *a standard political science text.*

In recent years, there have been several distinguished Polish Americans serving in Congress. Barbara Mikulski, a Democratic senator from Maryland, has helped rekindle Polish-American pride. She has argued for an integrated approach to ethnicity:

> Because of old prejudices and new fears, anger is generated against other minority groups rather than those who have power. What is needed is an alliance of white and black; white collar, blue collar, and no collar based on mutual need, interdependence and respect, and alliance to develop . . . a new kind of community organization and political participation.

Mikulski has been especially active in issues of concern to women, funding medical studies of diseases that affect women and working to end sexual harassment. As chairman of the House Ways and Means Committee, Polish-

American Dan Rostenkowski, a Chicago Democrat, was largely responsible for writing the tax reform bill of 1987. Another Polish American, Frank Murkowski, has represented the state of Alaska as a senator since 1980.

Polish Americans have long composed a large segment of the working community, and some members of the group have risen to high positions within the ranks of organized labor. Joseph "Jock" Yablonski, the United Mine Workers' insurgent candidate for union president in 1969, embodied the organization's growing reformist beliefs. When Yablonski lost his campaign for UMW president in a disputed election, he filed a complaint with the U.S. Department of Labor, alleging some 100 election violations. He then threatened to sue the incumbent president, Tony Boyle. But the trial never occurred: on New Year's Eve, 1970, Yablonski, his wife, Margaret, and their daughter, Charlotte, were shot to death by three hired gunmen. Boyle was later jailed for Yablonski's death.

Poets and Writers, Rebels and Intellectuals

Polish American intellectuals have greatly enriched the cultural life of their adopted country. One pioneering intellectual was Stephen Mizwa, who immigrated to the United States in 1910 and worked at a variety of menial jobs before pursuing an advanced education. He graduated from Amherst College, then earned a master's degree from Harvard. Mizwa became a teacher and in 1925 founded the Kosciuszko Foundation in New York City with the help of the president of Vassar College, Henry Noble MacCracken, and the president of Baldwin Locomotive Works, Samuel M. Vauvlain. The organization supports serious scholarship in Polish studies and encourages Polish-American youths to pursue intellectual achievement. The Kosciuszko Foundation's specific goals include:

> 1. To grant voluntary financial aid to deserving Polish students desiring to study at institutions of higher learning

in the United States of America; and to deserving American students hoping to study in Poland.

2. To encourage and aid the exchange of professors, scholars, and lecturers between Poland and the United States of America.

3. To cultivate closer intellectual and cultural relations between Poland and the United States in such ways and by which means as may from time to time seem wise, in the judgement of the Board of Directors of the Corporation.

The foundation subsidizes publication of works on Poland—including a number of doctoral dissertations—poetry readings, exhibits, concerts, and other cultural events. Since World War II, the organization has emphasized aiding refugee scholars from Poland; it also orga-

Czeslaw Milosz (left) received the Nobel Prize for literature from Sweden's King Karl Gustaf in 1980.

nizes summer programs in Polish language and culture at several Polish universities. These programs have allowed a new generation of Polish Americans to discover Poland's history and culture and to return to its roots.

During the 1950s and 1960s, a number of discontented intellectuals left Poland to make their home in North America. Among them was Czeslaw Milosz. Born in Lithuania in 1911, Milosz received his education in Poland. After World War II he entered the country's diplomatic corps. Stationed in Paris from 1945–50, he pursued a career as a writer, gaining a reputation in Europe for his poetry and prose. He came to the attention of American readers in 1953, with the English translation of *The Captive Mind,* a meditation on the plight of Polish writers forced to live under a Communist regime. In 1960 he immigrated to the United States and accepted a teaching job at the University of California. Ten years later, Milosz was naturalized, and 10 years after that he won the Nobel Prize for literature. His poetry, collected in *Selected Poems* (1972), *Bells in Winter* (1978), and other volumes, mingles lyrical imagery with penetrating insight. An accomplished prose writer, Milosz wrote an autobiographical novel, *The Issa Valley* (1981), which beautifully evokes the landscape of his youth, as well as *A Year of the Hunter* (1994), which is supposedly a year taken out of his diary.

The Polish-American writer W. S. Kuniczak is best known for his trilogy of novels about Poland during World War II, *The Thousand Hour Day* (1966), *The March* (1979), and *Valedictory* (1983). The son of a Polish army officer, Kuniczak was born in 1930 in Lwów, Poland, but he left his native land for Great Britain during the German-Soviet invasion of 1939. After earning a degree in political science from the London School of Economics, Kuniczak immigrated to the United States in 1950. He furthered his education at Alliance College (a now-defunct institution that was one of the few American colleges where a student could specialize in Polish

studies) and the Columbia School of Journalism and became a U.S. citizen in 1958. Stints in the army and as a reporter and editor with several newspapers preceded the completion of his first novel.

Most recently, Kuniczak has put his own projects on hold in order to serve a Polish literary master of the past, Henryk Sienkiewicz, who won the Nobel Prize for literature in 1905. Eighty-six years later, Kuniczak's English translation of *With Fire and Sword*, the first novel of Sienkiewicz's famed historical trilogy about 17th-century Poland, was hailed as a masterpiece on a par with the original, which has been characterized as the "greatest prose epic of Polish literature." *With Fire and Sword* was quickly followed by the last two volumes of Sienkiewicz's trilogy, *The Deluge* and *Fire in the Steppe*.

Poles in Entertainment

Poles have made great contributions to the screen, both the silver screen of Hollywood and the little screen of

In 1928, Gloria Swanson sits beside director Raoul Walsh during the filming of Sadie Thompson.

television. Pola Negri, Poland's first movie star, was born Appolonia Chalupec near the Polish town of Lipno in 1894. She made her debut in theater, then switched to the new medium of silent film, making her first appearance in a picture written and financed by herself, *Love and Passion* (1914). After starring in several more Polish films, she moved to Berlin and had a succession of hits, some directed by Ernst Lubitsch. He later went to Hollywood, as did Pola Negri, who became the first celluloid star to sign a contract with an American film company while working in Germany. In 1922 Negri arranged a meeting with the French tragedienne Sarah Bernhardt, at which she apologized for embarking on a Hollywood career at a time when movies were considered an inferior art to stage acting. The "divine

Sarah" replied, "Don't be apologetic. I would have done the same thing but I was too early." In America, Negri's dark beauty won her many roles as a temptress—or *femme fatale*—in *Bella Donna*, *The Cheat*, *The Spanish Dancer*, and others. Much admired by film critics, Negri is ranked alongside such silent-movie stars as Greta Garbo and Gloria Swanson. She died in 1987.

Gloria Swanson, also of Polish descent, was born in about 1898 in Chicago, the daughter of a civilian employee of the U.S. Army who raised her on military bases throughout the continent. As a teenager living in Chicago, Swanson acted in small parts with the Essanay studio located there. In 1916 she married Wallace Beery, one of the most popular film actors of the silent era, and accompanied him to Hollywood. There she landed steady work in comedies, but longed for serious dramatic roles. They came her way in 1918, when she starred in *Society for Sale*, *Her Decision*, and several other films. She then caught the eye of director Cecil B. de Mille, who cast her in major hits such as *Don't Change Your Husband* (1919) and *Why Change Your Wife?* (1920).

In the 1920s Swanson became one of Hollywood's reigning goddesses, known for her temperamental behavior and exotic wardrobes. The bill for her bridal garb in *Her Love Story* (1924) was said to have been $100,000. In 1925 Swanson found a new husband—a French count—and seemed more glamorous than ever. Her salary rose to gigantic proportions, exceeding $20,000 per week at a time when corporation executives earned perhaps twice that much in a year. With the arrival of talkies in 1927, Swanson's career foundered, not because she lacked a strong speaking voice but because a new generation of leading ladies had stolen the spotlight. She made a triumphant return to the screen in 1950, when she played aging movie star Norma Desmond in *Sunset Boulevard*.

Two of the most distinguished Polish-American film artists seldom appeared before the public. Joseph L.

Mankiewicz, born in 1909, was a producer, director, and scriptwriter who began his career as a journalist. His talent as a writer led him to Hollywood, where he produced such classics as *The Philadelphia Story* (1940) and *Woman of the Year* (1942), both starring Katharine Hepburn. In 1950 he directed *All About Eve*, which won the Academy Award for Best Picture and scored triumphs for Mankiewicz and star Bette Davis. Mankiewicz's brother Herman (1898–1953) also started his career in newspapers. He then went to Hollywood and wrote scripts, mostly comedies. In 1941, he won an Oscar for his screenplay for *Citizen Kane*, often called one of the best movies of all time. A celebrated wit, Mankiewicz made a remark about Orson Welles, *Citizen Kane*'s brilliant star and director, that later became film lore and is listed in *Bartlett's Familiar Quotations*. As Welles strolled through the set one day, enveloped in his own egotism, Mankiewicz muttered, "There but for the grace of God goes God."

Poland's most prominent contemporary filmmaker today is Andrzej Wajda. The films Wajda has made in Poland receive critical praise all over the world, though his themes—which probe sensitive areas of the Polish conscience—have incensed many of his compatriots. His film *Danton*, about the French Revolution, has been called an allegory of events occurring in Poland following the Solidarity strike. Another recent Wajda film, *A Love in Germany*, is a portrayal of the bureaucracy of the Nazi regime. Both these later films were shot in France.

Polish music has been brought to the American public by a number of popular singers, among them Bobby Vinton, "the Polish Prince." His huge hit in 1974, "My Melody of Love," was based on a Polish folk song and is sung partly in Polish. Vinton's other hits include "Roses are Red," "Blue on Blue," and "Blue Velvet." The entertainer had his own television show in the 1970s, and enjoys extreme popularity among the Polish-

American areas of the Midwest. Many of his songs are Polish, and he has even made an album that consists entirely of polkas.

Liberace, the flamboyant pianist and showman who died in 1987 of acquired immune deficiency syndrome (AIDS), also brought Polish music, including polkas, to American audiences. A virtuoso pianist who might have flourished on the classical concert stage, Liberace chose instead to popularize the music he loved with elaborate shows, outrageous costumes, and his trademark candelabra perched atop a grand piano.

In 1942, Stan Musial, shown here at the St. Louis Cardinals' spring training camp, was known to reporters as baseball's "golden boy."

Carl Yastrzemski was one of the few baseball players to collect 3,000 hits in a career. He played in more games than anyone in the history of the American League and was inducted into the Baseball Hall of Fame in 1989.

Sports Stars

In baseball—the most American of our national pastimes—Polish Americans have played brilliantly. Stan Musial, born in Donora, Pennsylvania, in 1920, became one of the top stars in National League history. Known to St. Louis Cardinal fans as Stan the Man, Musial won the Most Valuable Player award three times in a career that spanned 22 years, from 1941 to 1963. Elected to the Baseball Hall of Fame in 1969, he later served in the Cardinal's front office as a vice president.

Another Polish-American star, Carl Yastrzemski, was born in 1939 on the east end of Long Island, New York, where his grandfather owned a potato farm. Yastrzemski joined the Boston Red Sox in 1961, replacing retired Red Sox great Ted Williams, the last man to bat over .400 for an entire season. "Yaz" proved a worthy successor, becoming one of the best all-around players of his era. In 1967 he won the triple crown—leading the American league in batting average, home runs, and runs batted in—while powering the Red Sox to the World Series. His long career ended in 1983.

Other successful Polish-American ballplayers include Al Simmons, Tony Kubek, Greg "the Bull" Luzinski, Richie Zisk, Ted Kluszewski, Ed Lopat, Jim Konstanty, Ray Jablonski, Hank Majeski, George Shuba, Bill "Moose" Skowron, Ted Kazanski, Bob Kuzava, Cass Michaels, and Stan Lopata.

The people mentioned in this chapter are just a few of the prominent Polish Americans who have made significant contributions to their adopted homeland. One could easily cite many more, in a variety of fields: Professor Stanislaw Ulam of Harvard University, for example, who helped develop the atom bomb, the prominent architect Witold Rybczynski, who is also a best-selling author, or Tadeusz Sendzimir, whose inventions improved the processing of steel. Indeed, the contributions of Polish Americans are too many and too varied to sum up easily. Americans of Polish descent have entered into and become important in just about every aspect of American life. In the words of W. S. Kuniczak, the noted Polish-American novelist:

> There have been no significant movements in American history in which the Poles have not played a part, no area of American life in which they have not left an imprint of their own. They are a vital and energetic community of Americans, of many talents and considerable material resources, whose voice is only now beginning to be heard. ∾

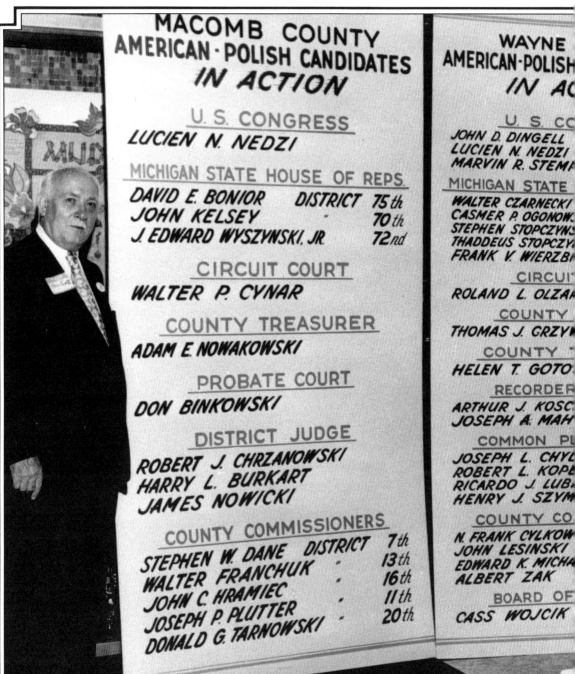

MACOMB COUNTY
AMERICAN-POLISH CANDIDATES
IN ACTION

U.S. CONGRESS
LUCIEN N. NEDZI

MICHIGAN STATE HOUSE OF REPS.
DAVID E. BONIOR   DISTRICT 75th
JOHN KELSEY   -   70th
J. EDWARD WYSZYNSKI, JR.   72nd

CIRCUIT COURT
WALTER P. CYNAR

COUNTY TREASURER
ADAM E. NOWAKOWSKI

PROBATE COURT
DON BINKOWSKI

DISTRICT JUDGE
ROBERT J. CHRZANOWSKI
HARRY L. BURKART
JAMES NOWICKI

COUNTY COMMISSIONERS
STEPHEN W. DANE   DISTRICT   7th
WALTER FRANCHUK   -   13th
JOHN C. HRAMIEC   -   16th
JOSEPH P. PLUTTER   -   11th
DONALD G. TARNOWSKI   20th

WAYNE
AMERICAN-POLISH
IN AC

U.S. CO
JOHN D. DINGELL
LUCIEN N. NEDZI
MARVIN R. STEMP

MICHIGAN STATE
WALTER CZARNECKI
CASMER P. OGONOW
STEPHEN STOPCZYNS
THADDEUS STOPCZY
FRANK V. WIERZBI

CIRCUI
ROLAND L. OLZA

COUNTY
THOMAS J. GRZYW

COUNTY
HELEN T. GOTO

RECORDER
ARTHUR J. KOSC
JOSEPH A. MAH

COMMON PL
JOSEPH L. CHYL
ROBERT L. KOPE
RICARDO J. LUB
HENRY J. SZYM

COUNTY CO
N. FRANK CYLKOW
JOHN LESINSKI
EDWARD K. MICHA
ALBERT ZAK

BOARD OF
CASS WOJCIK

THE VOICE OF POLONIA

A recently published history of Polish Americans by John J. Bukowczyk takes its title, *And My Children Did Not Know Me,* from a line in a Polish folk song whose lyrics lament the experience of too many Polish Americans:

When I journeyed from America . . .
And the foundry where I labored,
In pray'r my hands thanked our Father,
Hands that never shirked their labor.
Soon I came to New York City,
To the agent for my passage.
And the agents asked me if I
Had three hundred dollars with me.
"Ask me not such foolish questions.
For I carry gold and silver."
When I crossed the ocean midway,
No land could I see, sweet Virgin.
Our ship's captain was right busy,
Seeing, cheering all the people.
When I laid my eyes on Hamburg,
I thought I saw God Almighty.
When at last I landed safely,
"Lord," I prayed, "I thank thee for this.
O how grateful am I, dear God,
that I've crossed the ocean safely."
Berlin came next after Hamburg,

Members of the Alliance College faculty gather for a special convocation in 1972. Founded by the Polish National Alliance in 1912 to promote the study of Polish culture, the Pennsylvania college closed its doors in 1987.

"Barmaid, I will have some good wine."
Then I left Berlin for Krakow;
There my wife was waiting for me.
And my children did not know me,
For they fled from me, a stranger.
"My dear children, I'm your papa;
Three long years I have not seen you."

Remembering and Forgetting

A century ago, Poles who journeyed to America to start new lives worried about the curse of forgetfulness. They especially feared that their offspring would lose touch with the heritage of the homeland. Bukowcyzk's study quotes a letter written by a concerned immigrant sometime between 1876 and 1878:

> But what about the second, third and fourth generations? What of the children born of German, Irish, or American mothers? Sooner or later they will forget. They will change everything, even their names, which English teeth find too difficult to chew and which interfere with business. How long this will take is difficult to say. But just as Poland disappeared, so will this same sad fate inevitably befall her children who, today, are scattered throughout the world.

The author of this letter, Henryk Sienkiewicz, probably need not have fretted, for once the children of the original immigrants felt secure in American society, they tended to cling tenaciously to their heritage—even in the face of extreme prejudice.

Though not all immigrants went home to Poland, many retained tangible connections with the Old World, generally through friends or relatives still living in the old country. Often those who forsook Poland felt responsible for the well-being of those they left behind. Even today, the grandchildren of immigrants—people who think of themselves as American rather than Polish—send clothing and money to relatives they have never met. One third-generation Polish-American woman mailed "home" old clothing carefully lined with American cash—5- and 10-dollar bills that probably would have been confiscated if the Communist authorities discovered them.

Bukowcyzk also quotes an excerpt from "Why I Am Proud of My Polish Ancestry," an essay that won an award in a contest sponsored by *Reader's Digest* in the 1950s. At one point the essayist wrote:

Members of the Polish American Congress (PAC) protest Poland's Communist regime on the 30th anniversary of the Polish People's Republic. Since 1944, the PAC has been the leading political voice of the Polish-American community.

I am proud that I am a Pole—and for good reasons. My Polish ancestry entitles me to share in a history that is rich in God-fearing heroes and heroines, who have championed the cause of liberty, peace, and freedom; of honesty and justice; of equality and brotherhood. Polish descent offers a heritage of honor . . . YES, I am proud I am a Pole—for a good Pole has every right and reason to be a good American.

Rebirth

Recent events in Poland have reemphasized this "heritage of honor." Uprisings against the communists in

In 1983, Polish opposition leader Lech Walesa is cheered by fellow workers as he leaves the Gdansk shipyards.

1956, 1970, and 1976 attracted international attention, but while these rebellions led to some reforms (and the exile of many dissidents, several of whom emigrated to the United States) none decisively broke Communist power. But in August 1980, workers struck at the Lenin Shipyard in Gdansk, a city on the delta arm of the Vistula River in northern Poland. Soon, the striking workers were joined by laborers from other segments of the Polish economy, and the giant trade union Solidarity was born, under the leadership of Lech Walesa, an electrician at the Lenin Shipyard. In a short time, Solidarity became the powerful voice of the opposition in Poland, the strikes mounted in intensity, and the government increased its repression.

By December 1981, unrest was intensifying, the economy was in a shambles, and the Soviet Union was growing uneasy about what it viewed as the severest threat yet to the Communist regime it had imposed on Poland. One million of Poland's 3 million members of the Communist party had joined the ranks of Solidarity, but the Polish government, at the behest of the Soviets, refused to consider relinquishing any of its power to the opposition. On the morning of December 12, General Wojciech Jaruzelski, who had been appointed prime minister only the previous February, declared martial law, announcing that Poland was in a state of virtual war. Tanks rolled into the streets of Warsaw, Poland's capital, and the army erected roadblocks in several other cities. Hundreds of Solidarity activists, including Walesa, were arrested. Public meetings were forbidden, and independent groups and unions, Solidarity most conspicuous among them, were "suspended." After 500 heady days, its seemed the era of Solidarity had come to an end.

But Poles continued to resist. The opposition movement grew—aided, in no small part, by Poles in the United States. The Polish American Congress alone sent $122 million worth of relief goods to Poland

Playwright Janusz Glowacki is one of many Polish émigrés who have enriched the cultural life of the United States.

between 1981 and 1988. Smaller groups (many of them founded and run by exiled Solidarity organizers) smuggled money and equipment into the country to fund opposition newspapers and provide financial support for activists who had been jailed or lost their jobs as a result of their political beliefs.

In 1988, large-scale strikes broke out again in many of Poland's industrial centers, and in June 1989 the hitherto unthinkable occurred: free elections, the first in postwar Poland, resulted in humiliating setbacks for the communists, the accession of a Solidarity prime minister, and the creation of the first non-Communist government in the Soviet bloc. The next year, elections were held for Poland's presidency. In acknowledgement of the fact that many patriotic Poles had been forced out of their homeland by the communists, the Polish government allowed first-generation Polish immigrants living in the United States and Canada to vote even if they had accepted citizenship in their new countries. In November 1990, thousands of Poles living in the United States helped elect Lech Walesa as the president of Poland.

Polish Americans have continued to aid post-Communist Poland in its quest to develop a stable economy. The Polish government has embraced the policy of dismantling state-owned businesses and industries and encouraging private investment and enterprise. To ensure the success of this policy, Polish Americans lobbied the U.S. Congress to pass the Support for Eastern European Democracy Act of 1989, which included more than $840 million in aid earmarked for Poland. In addition, Polish Americans have formed the Polish-American Enterprise Fund, which provides small businesses in Poland with loans and advice, and Tokten (Transfer of Knowledge Through Expatriate Nationals), which places Polish-American business and legal advisers in Poland.

Immigrants and Exiles

Although some of the dissidents who left Poland while it was under Communist rule returned after the 1989 elections, others had built new lives in the United States and chose to remain. While these new immigrants had been involved in a variety of occupations in Poland, most of them came from the cities, and many were members of Poland's intelligentsia who felt stifled by the repressions of the Soviet regime. In the United States they often congregated in cultural communities alongside artists and other exiles seeking greater freedom. One such émigré, New Yorker Janusz Glowacki, received critical acclaim for his play *Hunting Cockroaches*, which concerns the immigrant experience. Glowacki told the *New York Times* that waiting for reviews in Communist Poland was

Polish filmmaker Zbigniew Rybczynski won an Academy Award for best animated short subject for his film Tango *in 1983.*

different from waiting for them in the United States. In Poland a good review in the official paper (distrusted by intellectuals) often meant no one would show up to see the play. "But a very bad review in the official press could cause a line in front of the theatre the very next day."

Another recent immigrant is filmmaker Zbigniew Rybczynski, whose remarkable short film *Tango* (made in Poland) won an Oscar. His films, generally shorts and usually animated, masterfully portray the repetitiveness and constraints of life in a repressive society. Rybczynski made numerous films in Poland—he was given the money and the equipment to do so in order to fulfill the government-owned studio's quota—but his best films were banned until 1989 in his homeland. Through the early 1990s, he continued to make films, including several features that were shown at the New York Film Festival, as well as a number of music videos.

The Old System

Despite these changes, other Poles still venture to North America for the same reason their forebears did a century ago: to make money quickly and then return home.

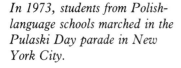

In 1973, students from Polish-language schools marched in the Pulaski Day parade in New York City.

One such immigrant, Witold Wroblewski, met a fate that sums up the conflicting sides of the American experience. In 1986 he arrived in New York City with the intention of earning enough money to pay for an operation needed by his paralyzed son. Wroblewski had been working for eight months at a gas station in Riverhead, Long Island, when robbers held up the place. They shot at a glass door, sending shards of glass and bullets into Wroblewski's face. Luckily, he survived, and his wife and ailing son were able to join him in the United States. Concerned New Yorkers raised $80,000 for the operation that will help 7-year-old Wojtek Wroblewski walk again.

The G train carries Polish Americans from their neighborhood in Greenpoint, Brooklyn, to the wider world of metropolitan New York.

An Old-Style Neighborhood

As late as 1992, a large community of Polish immigrants lived in Greenpoint, a neighborhood in the New York City borough of Brooklyn. Its main thoroughfare, Manhattan Avenue, seems transported from Warsaw or Cracow. The employees in the supermarket still converse in Polish and many small shops have hand-lettered signs written in Polish. Clothiers selling Polish furs—hats and coats—nestle up against travel agencies offering discount plane tickets to the homeland. Wedding parties often celebrate at the local community center, then feast at one of the nearby ethnic restaurants, which specialize in treats such as pickled herring, stuffed golabki, and *kielbasa*—Polish sausage. The neighborhood's Catholic churches include large stone structures built of gray stone and smaller buildings built of clapboard glossed with shiny white paint.

Many of Greenpoint's Polish Americans live on the quiet streets that empty into or parallel Manhattan Avenue. Here two- and three-story apartment buildings— erected a century ago as single-family dwellings—sport new exteriors made of composition shingle or aluminum siding. Today these apartments accommodate several families who inhabit "railroad" or "dumbbell" apartments—long narrow flats broken up into connecting rooms that afford no privacy and little light. Many of the apartments serve as a sort of dormitory for single men—usually immigrants just arrived from Poland and too poor to rent entire apartments for themselves. These immigrants pay a monthly fee for sleeping space—a cot crammed alongside several others. In the building's foyer a visitor will sometimes see six or seven different names taped to a mailbox meant to serve a single family.

Greenpoint attracts so many Polish immigrants because the existing community helps them adjust to life in the United States. Jobs often await men in a nearby glass factory, and many women ride the subway to Manhattan where they work in the evenings cleaning large office buildings. On Saturday night, newcomers join more established Polish Americans in the neighborhood's eateries and pubs or convene for political discussions in the local outpost of Solidarity. On Sundays, Polish Americans of different generations, clad in suits and fine dresses, fill the pews of Greenpoint's churches.

Recent events have caused many Polish Americans to renew their ties with Poland. The story of Solidarity reminds Polish Americans of their connection to an ancestral homeland; it also reminds them that they are lucky to have found a nation that has granted them the opportunity denied them in Poland. In the years to come Poles will undoubtedly continue to view the United States as a haven of freedom and democracy, just as they did two centuries ago. In the future, more Poles will probably leave behind a familiar life for the possibilities offered by America, and they will enrich an ethnic community that has already made a lasting mark on the larger society that contains it. ✎

FURTHER READING

Bukowczyk, John J. *And My Children Did Not Know Me: A History of the Polish-Americans.* Bloomington, IN: Indiana University Press, 1987.

Davies, Norman. *Heart of Europe: A Short History of Poland.* New York: Oxford University Press, 1986.

Kuniczak, W. S. *My Name Is Million: An Illustrated History of the Poles in America.* New York: Doubleday, 1978.

Mocha, Frank, ed. *Poles in America: Bicentennial Essays.* Stevens Point, WI: Worzalla Publishing Co., 1978.

Polish American Historical Association. *Polish American Studies.* Chicago, IL.

Renkiewicz, Frank. *The Poles in America 1608–1972: A Chronology and Fact Book.* Dobbs Ferry, NY: Oceana Publications Inc., 1973.

Thomas, William I., and Florian Znaniecki. *The Polish Peasant in Europe and America.* Volume II. New York: Dover, 1958.

Wrobel, Paul. *Our Way: Family, Parish, and Neighborhood in a Polish-American Community.* Notre Dame, Indiana: University of Notre Dame Press, 1979.

Wtulich, Josephine. *Writing Home: Immigrants in Brazil and the United States 1890-1891.* Boulder, CO: East European Monographs, 1986.

Wytrwal, Joseph A. *Behold! The Polish Americans.* Detroit: Endurance Press, 1977.

INDEX

PICTURE CREDITS

SANDRA STOTSKY is director of the Institute on Writing, Reading, and Civic Education at the Harvard Graduate School of Education as well as a research associate there. She is also editor of *Research in the Teaching of English,* a journal sponsored by the National Council of Teachers of English.

Dr. Stotsky holds a bachelor of arts degree with distinction from the University of Michigan and a doctorate in education from the Harvard Graduate School of Education. She has taught on the elementary and high school levels and at Northeastern University, Curry College, and Harvard. Her work in education has ranged from serving on academic advisory boards to developing elementary and secondary curricula as a consultant to the Polish Ministry of Education. She has written numerous scholarly articles, curricular materials, encyclopedia entries, and reviews and is the author or co-author of three books on education.

MARY BARR SISSON has an A.B. in English and American Language and Literature from Harvard-Radcliffe University. She currently lives in Queens, New York, and works as a writer and editor.

REED UEDA is associate professor of history at Tufts University. He graduated summa cum laude with a bachelor of arts degree from UCLA, received master of arts degrees from both the University of Chicago and Harvard University, and received a doctorate in history from Harvard.

Dr. Ueda was research editor of the *Harvard Encyclopedia of American Ethnic Groups* and has served on the board of editors for *American Quarterly, Harvard Educational Review, Journal of Interdisciplinary History,* and *University of Chicago School Review.* He is the author of several books on ethnic studies, including *Postwar Immigrant America: A Social History, Ethnic Groups in History Textbooks,* and *Immigration.*

DANIEL PATRICK MOYNIHAN is the senior United States senator from New York. He is also the only person in American history to serve in the cabinets or subcabinets of four successive presidents—Kennedy, Johnson, Nixon, and Ford. Formerly a professor of government at Harvard University, he has written and edited many books, including *Beyond the Melting Pot, Ethnicity: Theory and Experience* (both with Nathan Glazer), *Loyalties,* and *Family and Nation.*

SEAN DOLAN has a degree in American history from the State University of New York. He has written and edited many history books for young adults.